CW00944453

Squash
R U L E S

Squash
RULES

ANDREW SHELLEY

WARD LOCK

A WARD LOCK BOOK

First published in the UK 1997
by Ward Lock
Wellington House
125 Strand
LONDON
WC2R 0BB

A Cassell Imprint

Copyright © Ward Lock 1997

All rights reserved. No part of this publication
may be reproduced in any material form
(including photocopying or storing it in any
medium by electronic means and whether or
not transiently or incidentally to some other
use of this publication) without the written
permission of the copyright owner, except in
accordance with the provisions of the
Copyright, Designs and Patents Act 1988 or
under the terms of licence issued by the
Copyright Licensing Agency, 90 Tottenham
Court Road, London W1P 9HE. Applications for
the copyright owner's written permission to
reproduce any part of this publication should
be addressed to the publisher.

Distributed in the United States by
Sterling Publishing Co., Inc.
387 Park Avenue South, New York,
NY 10016-8810

A British Library Cataloguing in Publication
Data block for this book may be obtained from
the British Library

ISBN 0 7063 7602 1

Printed and bound in Great Britain by
Hillman Printers (Frome) Ltd, Somerset

ACKNOWLEDGEMENT

The author would like to thank David Donelly,
Director of the World Squash Federation Rules
Committee, for painstakingly checking the text
in his inimitable style. His attention to detail
should ensure that it reflects both the wording
and intent of the *Rules of Squash*.

Cover Rodney Eyles (right) v. Chris Walker at
the 1996 Super Series Finals.

Frontispiece Top Australian player Rodney
Eyles may be making too physical an
attempt to get past Jansher Khan to reach
the ball. Or didn't Jansher make enough
effort to get out of the way?

CONTENTS

INTRODUCTION

Squash has been likened to tennis . . . but with both players on the same side of the net. To a certain extent this is fair, but squash has one fundamental ingredient that tennis doesn't – shots can be played after a ball has hit a court wall. In tennis it will simply smack into the court surrounds, and be called 'out'.

If you haven't played squash, imagine that two people are in a large rectangular box trying to trade shots which hit the wall in front of them. As in tennis, the ball must be hit before it bounces twice, but it is the option of hitting the ball after it has hit various walls, and onto any wall (as long as it hits the front wall before the floor) that is a major delight for squash devotees.

Even as a beginner, the huge variety of angles that you can use will both enthral and frustrate you. Then, as you progress, you will not only consider the angles but also work towards sending the ball into one of the floor

and wall joins (called 'nicks') to make it difficult or, sometimes, satisfyingly impossible for your opponent to return it and so continue the rally.

Not surprisingly, there are complications to the game, and while this book is not aiming to teach the sport, much of what you need to know in order to play effectively stems from understanding the rules, ensuring that you don't place yourself at a disadvantage. As certain aspects are covered, so your tactical under-standing should be enhanced.

Over 50 years ago a British Open Squash Champion wrote that the history of squash 'is wrapped in mystery'. Since then, there has still been no definitive study to pinpoint its beginnings, but the sport evolved from the ball games played in different-sized, though defined, areas into the game of rackets. Rackets is the most recent forebear of squash, and the game from which much of the squash rules, terminology, court markings and marker's calls clearly derive.

Order was achieved as rules were developed in the early decades of the 1900s, but they, together with the materials for court, balls and rackets, have continued to evolve. Older players will remember wooden squash rackets that were common until the mid-1980s, but younger ones will probably never have seen one of those. In recent years, transparent courts have become available, and have been erected in various locations around the world for the major championships. They have brought with them coloured floors and walls, together with white squash balls.

Although squash is primarily a participant sport, it strives to become more attractive to television viewers as it tries to market itself. Not only has this led to rule and presentational changes to help encourage the process, but has also given you, the player, the opportunity to see the professionals plying their trade. However, when you see these matches, it is a good idea to take note of the decisions of the referee as well as watching the players. If you can position yourself on a similar line of

The introduction of squash courts with glass back walls opened up a whole range of viewing positions for spectators.

sight to that of the match officials, this should give you an insight into their decision-making. See if their verdicts match your own assessments.

The *Rules of Squash* have become very long and make very dry reading. They attempt to be comprehensive, and are written in a way that, although it may be uninteresting, tries to minimize ambiguity. They are also aimed very much at officials, and so large tracts cover refereeing and marking aspects related to competitive play. While these are not entirely irrelevant, they go beyond what is necessary for most club players.

Of course, as a recreational player it is perfectly possible to play for a lifetime without ever reading the *Rules*

Would you want to referee a match when you have a thousand or more 'spectator referees' also arbitrating on the same game?

of Squash. However, to do so will lessen your own enjoyment and that of those with whom you play. If you buy an electrical appliance, for example, you can possibly muddle through without reading the instructions, but this is hardly the best approach.

This book attempts to pinpoint the fundamentals of the *Rules* in terms that will be understood by all players. It is not a definitive guide to every single rule, but covers those that you really should know, and offers background information on how they link with each other.

Whatever your standard of play, find a corner of your squash bag for this book. You will then be in a position to resolve questions that have arisen when you have played, even if you don't recall all of the rules following your initial reading.

Remember – the rules have been developed with the twin aims of ensuring that a fair result can be achieved and that the sport is played in as safe a manner as possible. This book will help you towards both, when you are on the court as well as off the court.

 **NOTES**

For grammatical convenience only, 'he, his and him' have been used throughout to refer to both sexes.

The *Rules of Squash* are amended every four years by the World Squash Federation. In October 1996 changes were made (which come into effect from 1 May 1997) and these are incorporated in this book. The rules should not be subject to any further alteration until 2001.

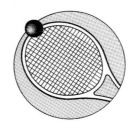

THE COURT AND EQUIPMENT

Most sports have their own jargon, and squash is no exception. 'Lets', where rallies are replayed, are universally understood by players, and there are several other terms which will appear. However, since the court itself has names for its component parts, these are listed below for clarity.

● PARTS OF THE COURT

Back Wall – the wall (lowest), at the rear of the court

Board – the name for the strip which sits on the top of the tin at the base of the front wall

Front Wall – the wall onto which the ball is played, above the tin

Half court line – the line which divides the back half of the floor into two quarters for service placement, the front end of which forms the 'T' with the short line

Lines – lines on a wall define borders of area, so a ball hitting them will be 'down', 'out' or a fault, as appropriate

Nicks – the corners where walls or walls and floor meet

Out line – the line which goes around the top of the four walls of the court

Service box – the small boxes at either end of the short line from which the server serves

Service line – the horizontal line on the front wall above which every service must be hit

Short line – the line which divides the front and back portions of the court and beyond which, towards the back, the served ball must reach.

Side wall lines – the sloping lines on each side of the court

The 'T' – the point in the centre of the court where the short line meets the half court line.

Tin – The area that is at the base of the front wall

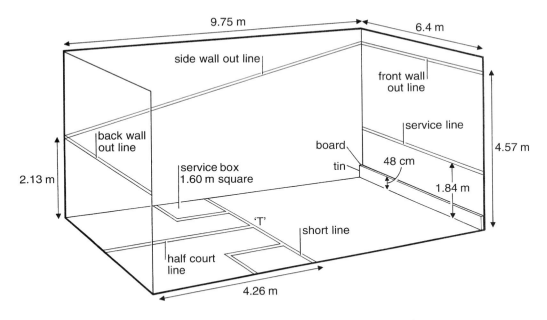

9.75 m

6.4 m

side wall out line

front wall
out line

service line

back wall
out line

board

4.57 m

48 cm

service box
1.60 m square

tin

2.13 m

1.84 m

'T'

short line

half court
line

4.26 m

Dimensions of a squash court.

● THE SQUASH BALL

Like that of the game itself, the history of the squash ball is one of evolution. Now, after various materials and sizes were tried in the early years of the sport, we are left with a standardized butyl ball. Ordinary rubber is mixed with butyl, a synthetic substance, in various levels to produce the hollow halves, which are bonded together. While there are several manufacturers of squash balls, a measure of uniformity is achieved since the World Squash Federation publishes specifications for squash balls. These include the diameter, the weight and how bouncy they should be.

There are four speeds of ball (indicated by the colour of the dot printed on them.) They are: blue dot (fast), red dot (medium), white dot (slow) and yellow dot (extra slow.) The descriptions of speed relate to how bouncy they are. Therefore a blue dot is especially lively, and ideal for beginners, while at the other end of the spectrum the yellow dot is much less 'zingy' and will be used by better players and in tournament play.

Match balls are almost invariably black, but other colours are produced, with green being widely used by recreational players. If you watch a championship played on a transparent court, however, you will see the players hitting a white ball (with a yellow dot!). This is the equivalent of a black extra slow, but white shows up better against the coloured walls, which are a feature of these transportable championship courts.

Choice

Assuming that both players have a ball in their squash bag a choice may need to be made between them – as opposed to a club league match or tournament where one will normally be supplied. While you would normally use a yellow-dot ball, it is not necessary to adhere slavishly to this norm if the court is cold. If there is a difference of opinion between you and your playing partner, then use the yellow-dot except in particularly cold courts, as a ball that doesn't bounce will not provide an enjoyable playing session.

When the ball is not in actual play, if both players agree, another ball can be substituted during the match, if the initial one is found to be too bouncy or too slow.

Warm-up

There is a five-minute allowance for the warm-up at the start of the match, to enable the ball to reach playing temperature and the muscles and joints of the players to flex. Normally the two players change sides of the court halfway through this period. If both players are ready, though, there is no obligation to use the full five

minutes, and certainly in friendly matches very often the full time allocation is not used. Also, if the players agree, the ball can be briefly warmed again at the start of any game.

In fact, one of the regularly abused etiquettes of the game is for a player to hit the ball back to himself three or four or even more times in a row before hitting across again to his opponent. This is both frustrating to the opponent and very unsporting. (From a tactical perspective, you should use the warm-up to seek out the weaker shots of your opponent, but it becomes somewhat difficult if you don't hit the ball to him!) Therefore if you are refereeing you can step in, if necessary, to ensure that both players are able to warm up both themselves and the ball.

At the end of the warm-up, a player may leave the court, possibly to remove his tracksuit, but if he does depart he must return within the maximum 90-second interval allowable between the warm-up and the start of the match.

Breaking during play

If the ball breaks during play then a let is played on the rally that is in progress. However, if the break was not noticed during the rally but is found *before* the server starts the next rally, then a let for the preceding rally is still played.

A player may stop mid-rally because he believes the ball to be broken. If it turns out that it isn't, then he loses the uncompleted rally, so it is best to continue to the end of the rally and then inspect it.

If a player suspects that the ball has burst in the last rally of the game, then he must check (as the referee would do if there is an appeal) before the players leave the court. After this juncture there can be no appeal.

When a new ball is used following a breakage, the players are permitted to warm it up to playing temperature. Play can recommence when the players agree that the ball has become lively enough.

● RACKETS, CLOTHING AND SHOES

As you might expect, there are detailed racket and clothing specifications published by the World Squash Federation. These aim to provide players and manufacturers alike with guidance as to what is acceptable.

In terms of rackets, when you buy a squash racket made by a reputable manufacturer you will know that it conforms to the various minimum and maximum stipulations made in terms of length, width, stringing area, etc. Your concern will be whether its weight and balance suit you – for there is quite a range of weights (normally falling within a 140–190g band), and each will have this weight distributed slightly more or less towards head or handle. Try them, get advice, and you should find one that suits you.

In the context of safety, however, you will need to keep an eye on your racket, just in case the bumper strip around the head has become gashed somehow and there is a sharpened protrusion from it. This could lead to an injury if you were to catch your opponent with it, so simply shave it off as a preventative measure. You should also renew your grip regularly, as a worn grip makes the racket much more likely to slip from your hand, and possibly hit your opponent.

The rules also detail what clothing can be worn in championships, but since much of this relates to advertising area it is not applicable for recreational play. Essentially, you should be looking for clothing that has been produced for indoor sports use, so that it allows flexibility of movement, and can deal with perspiration.

Shoe types are not covered by the rules, but most clubs insist on non-marking soles. This essentially means light-coloured ones. However, to help absorb the pounding that the joints take when you rush around and jump, not to wear shoes designed for squash use would be folly indeed. Good support and padding are essential.

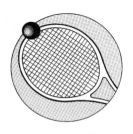

THE SCORING SYSTEM AND TIME ALLOWANCES

Virtually all squash is played to the best of five games, which means the first player to reach three games wins the match.

Each game is scored to nine points, except when the score reaches eight all. At this point the non-server can decide whether to play the remainder of the game to nine (calling 'set one') or ten ('set two'). The game then concludes when the first player reaches the nominated total. (NB It is not necessary to have a two-point margin, i.e. 10–8, as when 'two' is called 10–9 is a possible result.)

● SCORING POINTS

Points can only be won by the player who is serving. When he loses a rally, known as 'hand out', the other player serves and scores points until he loses a rally. This is undoubtedly one of the greatest attractions of the sport at recreational level, because fortunes can ebb and flow without points totals running away, as they are more likely to do when points are scored irrespective of serve. It also gives rise to players often being able to stage a fightback when they are down in a game, as the one who is ahead can become defensive and lose the initiative.

Point-a-rally scoring (PARS) is used for doubles, handicap events and, at present, for some men's professional matches (on an experimental basis). In this form of scoring, points are scored irrespective of who is serving. Games are played to 15 points. If the game reaches 14 all, the non-server chooses whether the game is played to 15 (set one) or 17 points (set three).

PARS began to be used by professionals in an attempt to shorten matches, and so reduce wear and tear to their overtrained joints. However, subsequently, the emphasis changed to the suggestion that it may be more exciting for viewing – after it was found not to actually reduce the length of matches at the top level. This also has not been proven, because, while play builds nicely towards double figures, it can then become more defensive as the crisis end of the game is looming closer. Experiments with other different formats are also occasionally tried at professional events.

● TIME PERIODS

There are several time periods stipulated in the rules, including:

- Warm-up – 5 minutes' duration (maximum) (2½ minutes each side)
- Between warm-up and start – 90 seconds maximum
- Between games – 90 seconds
- Before end of interval between games – 15 seconds (call by referee to let players know that they should be nearly ready to resume)
- Changing equipment – 90 seconds
- Illness/injury – see pp. 51–2.

Included within the changing equipment section would be various problems such as a player losing his

contact lenses or his glasses breaking. In those instances, players are allowed to use the designated time to resolve their difficulty.

● TIME-WASTING

'Play shall be continuous' is one of the main principles of the rules. Referees will warn players if they consider that they are wasting time, and this form of conduct is not acceptable even without a referee being present. Quite simply, it is an unfair attempt to gain advantage or respite.

Always avoid:

- wandering around before serving
- standing to get your breath back
- changing your mind as to where to serve from
- repeatedly bouncing the ball before serving
- tying your shoelaces repeatedly
- pretending to be injured
- discussing the score etc with the opponent to delay play.

Other variations that have been used include deliberately kicking the ball away, knocking it out of court, repeatedly blowing the nose, and lifting imaginary fluff off the floor. None has any place in squash.

At a simplistic level, you may say that having paid for your time slot on court you should use all of it, but, more importantly, the spirit of the

rules and the game itself should not be abused.

Another point to be mentioned here is that if you legitimately need to leave the court to change racket, clothing or footwear you may do so as quickly as you can, and within the maximum 90 seconds allowable for changing equipment. Where a match has a referee, he will need to give his

A maximum interval of 90 seconds is available between games to rest and collect your thoughts.

permission before you do so. Should you exceed this time, or not be back on court after the referee calls 'Time' at the at the end of the interval between games, then the referee can warn or penalize you.

SERVING AND RALLYING

At the start of each match the two players spin a racket to decide who serves. Normally this is determined by one player guessing whether a mark or letter on the frame will be the right way up or upside down when the racket falls.

● WHICH SERVICE BOX?

The player who has gained the right to serve first can choose to start from either service box. He then alternates boxes every time he wins ensuing rallies. When his opponent wins service he also chooses where to start, then alternates. The incoming server can always start from whichever side he wishes. Most players usually begin serving from the right box (unless they are playing a left-hander), in a bid to

serve to the backhand first, but there is no obligation to do so.

Should you serve from the wrong box, and the mistake is realized after the rally begins, then the rally continues until its conclusion and the game carries on as if no error had been made. Do not try to put it right by serving from the same box three times in a row. (This should not happen if a referee is present, because he will make sure that the correct box is used.)

If a rally ends in a let, the server must begin play again from the same box from which he started the unfinished rally.

For all games after the first one, if you are in the happy position of having won the preceding game, you will have the right to serve to start the next game.

THE SERVICE ITSELF

So, how do you serve, not in a tactical sense, but in terms of a serve that is acceptable within the rules? As with all aspects of the game, the rules are quite comprehensive with regard to the service. They even cover a dispensation for a one-armed player who cannot toss the ball. The general principles that you must know and adhere to are:

- **the ball** must be tossed into the air, or dropped from the hand or racket, and hit directly onto the front wall above the service line and below the out line
- **the ball** must not bounce on the floor or hit the side wall when tossed or dropped before it is hit
- **the ball** must bounce in the

opposite rear quarter if the opponent does not volley it back

- **one foot** (or part of it) must be touching the floor inside the service box, without it touching the line. The other foot of the server may be outside the box (otherwise it is termed a 'footfault').

The rules make no stipulation about service action, so you can serve underarm, sidearm, or overarm as long as you fulfil all the requirements. If you do not hit the ball correctly as above, or the service is otherwise not good (see p. 20) then your opponent can serve as the rally is deemed to be lost. You don't get a second go.

Opposite Top woman player Liz Irving has one foot touching the floor inside the service box, and not the line.

Below As long as one foot is completely in the service box, the other can be touching the floor outside.

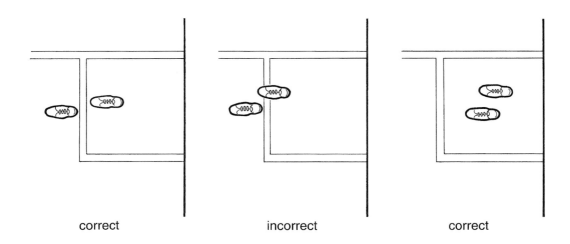

correct   incorrect   correct

● SERVICE PROBLEMS

The most common problem area regarding the service is whether the server has served above the service line. If, as receiver, you are doubtful, suggest playing a let. If you, as server, think that the ball has hit the line (or the wall below it, of course) then call your own service a fault.

Other instances in which a service is not good are when:

- the ball strikes any line, goes out, or does not return to the correct quarter court
- the ball hits a side wall or the join between side and front (the 'nick') before hitting the front wall
- the server misses the ball entirely when he attempts to serve (however, if the server is unhappy with the toss, or for any other reason does not attempt to strike the ball, he may do so again)
- the server strikes the ball with a double hit on the racket.

Note: If a fault is served, the receiver cannot accept it and continue the rally. Serving a fault leads to automatic loss of serve.

Finally, the 'corkscrew serve' is a hard-hit serve which strikes high where the front and side wall join before 'corkscrewing' across to the diagonal back corner. Because it has to be hit hard it can be quite difficult to determine whether it has hit the side wall or the front wall first, but if it is the side wall first then it is a fault.

● THE RALLY

If your service is good, and your opponent returns it to the front wall (either directly, or via side or back wall) before it has bounced twice on the floor, the rally progresses until one of you is unable to make a return, or the rally is undecided and so requires a stroke or let decision to be made. In playing terms we might talk of finishing a rally by hitting a 'winner', or the opponent making an error, but in more specific form the rally will end if the ball:

- bounces more than once
- hits the tin (before or after touching the front wall)
- touches the floor before reaching the front wall
- hits the out line or the area above it
- touches the clothing or body of the striker
- hits the striker's racket again (double hit)
- touches the body, clothing or racket of the opponent.

As squash rules are sometimes a little complicated, there are a few additional aspects that need to be borne in mind:

- the ball when hit can, of course, hit either side or back wall before or after hitting the front wall (except when serving), but it must reach the front wall before bouncing on the floor
- the racket must be in your hand when you hit the ball, i.e. you cannot throw the racket at the ball in a desperate attempt to reach it
- you must not catch the ball after you have hit it against the front wall before it bounces twice, assuming that your opponent would not have reached it (e.g. if your opponent slips over after having hit the ball and could not possibly get up in time to reach your response, were you to catch the ball after it has hit the front wall it would actually be a stroke to your fallen opponent)
- in addition to a double hit, a player is not allowed to play a shot where the ball rests on the strings fractionally longer than the normal momentary strike – called a 'scoop' (an example of this may be a 'shovelled' shot from the back of the court where the ball is carried up and over on the racket).

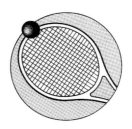

ETIQUETTE, SAFETY AND PLAYERS' OBLIGATIONS

As an overwhelming proportion of squash matches do not have a referee it is the responsibility of the players to keep score and make necessary decisions between them . . . and to do so amicably. Only a tiny fraction of players compete for a living. The rest, if asked, say that they play for fun. If fun equates to enjoyment, not a great deal will be had if disputes punctuate the course of a match.

Yet, despite the importance of the rules and of general etiquette and safety considerations, there is no general policy among clubs and centres that new members should be introduced to both of these aspects of the game at the same time as meeting some of their fellow members. Worse still are pay-as-you-play centres, where learning only comes if you are fortunate enough to have games against an experienced opponent who takes the time to explain.

● SQUASH ETIQUETTE

If you have ever stood in a squash club bar, you will probably have heard somebody being discussed in disparaging terms. His knowledge of the rules and general behaviour on court are the object of much displeasure. Nobody relishes playing such a person, and some actually won't do so, preferring to forfeit the points in the monthly league. But just reflect . . . do they in fact talk about you like that?

Foremost among possible areas of disagreement are situations where there might be uncertainty whether a player is entitled to the fulsome award of a stroke, just a let, or nothing at all. The onus is on every player to adopt a sensible and tolerant view of the proceedings. Where reasonable, give your opponent the benefit of the doubt, even to your own disadvantage, if it means the game is more likely to come to an uncontentious end. If you feel your opponent is entitled to a let (where the point is replayed) or a stroke (where a point is awarded to an impeded player), offer one. Don't wait for it to be requested. If you feel that he has got more than he deserved (a stroke when you felt it was a let, for example) don't let it rankle, but simply adopt a slightly more tight interpretation when the situation is reversed and you are asking.

Of course there will be occasions when players disagree, but if you have read and understood the rules, then you will be able to offer a concise reason for your view. It may not be always be accepted, but it is more likely than not to defuse the situation and allow the game to proceed. You may also be doing your opponent a favour by educating him!

Understanding the rules of squash thoroughly will not only improve your game, but also enable you to handle matches when asked to referee, and give you confidence on court that you are dealing with strokes, lets and no lets properly as you play.

Doubles squash is not for the fainthearted or inexperienced player!

● SAFETY CONSIDERATIONS

The *Rules of Squash* have two fundamental principles as their bedrock. Not surprisingly, one is to bring about a fair result to the match, but the other, equally important, is to try to ensure the safety of both players.

Squash is basically two (or, in doubles, four) players swinging rackets to zing a projectile around a small room. While players instinctively will try not to allow themselves to get too close to their opponent's racket, and will take evasive action if they sense that the ball is coming towards them, there is an ever-present element of danger. To minimize this, players have specific obligations:

- never attempt to make contact with the ball if there is a danger of the ball or your racket hitting your opponent
- keep your swing as compact as possible

The incoming player can expect his opponent to clear his shot, but only after he has finished playing it.

- don't crowd your opponent when he is playing the ball
- make every effort to get out of the way of your opponent
- give your opponent all the front wall to aim at.

As you will see in later sections, a let (or sometimes a stroke) will always be available to you if, as the incoming striker, you refrain from striking the ball if there is any danger that your racket or the ball will hit your opponent.

After hitting the ball, it is your responsibility to get out of the way to give your opponent access to move to the ball, room to swing and the full front wall to aim at. One of the best ways of doing this is by thinking of one of the really basic precepts of playing squash, i.e. in virtually all circumstances hit the ball away from yourself even before thinking next about keeping it away from your opponent. The logic of this is that you can hardly give away a stroke if the ball, and so your opponent, are not near you. For example, following your opponent's drop shot with one of your own will inevitably lead to a stroke against you if you hit the ball in front of you when your opponent is close by.

The rules cover the increasing degrees of interference, as it is called, and there is also scope within the rules to deal with intentional blocking. However, since this is a fundamental breach of both fair play and the spirit of the game, any player attempting this will be dealt with severely by a referee in officiated matches, and find himself without any opponents before long at club level.

Finally, a couple of general don'ts that will help to avoid the possibility of injury:

- don't hit the ball after the end of the rally, as your opponent may not be expecting you to do so
- once a let has been called for, stop play immediately.

● PLAYERS' OBLIGATIONS

It is up to both players to play their part to allow the game to flow smoothly and be played as safely as possible. The pivotal point here is player 'traffic' on court. Clearly rallies are much more likely to end with a winning shot or an error being squeezed from the opponent if the two players are not getting in each other's way. Naturally. the space between them will also lessen their chances of hitting each other with racket and ball.

While this utopia is not possible to achieve at even the highest level, it can be striven for most effectively by always having the fundamental thought in your mind that you will be trying to play the ball away from yourself, as well as out of reach of your opponent. Couple this with good

tangential movement back to the centre of the court (as taught by coaches), rather than straight-line runs, and the number of longer, satisfying rallies will definitely increase.

Let's discuss these principles in a little more detail. Essentially, each player has to give the opponent:

- a fair view of the ball
- direct access to reach it
- freedom of swing
- a clear front wall at which to strike.

Fair view

This means what it says – a reasonable sight of the ball. This is denied if the ball is hit back close to the striker after hitting the front wall, but only if the incoming player is in a position to reach the ball and would

This overhead shot shows how much room a player might reasonably need for a backswing on the backhand side.

hit the outgoing striker were he to play the ball directly to the front wall. Therefore, you will still win the rally if the ball passes back close to you but your opponent is not close enough to reach it in the first place. (These decisions are discussed on p. 33.)

You cannot make a claim, however, if you are unable to see the ball due to your own poor positioning, e.g. if you are caught behind a player who is hitting a drop shot from the middle or rear of the court. In this instance the opponent has not hit the ball back remotely close to himself, but you have got trapped behind him.

Direct access

Direct access to the ball is based around the requirement of a player making room for the opponent to move into position to play his shot by getting out of the way as soon as a shot has been completed. It seems a simple-enough principle, but in squash there are so many variations that can arise on court. To clear up one of these at the outset, if you do not make an effort to move out of the way (clear the ball), your opponent automatically wins the rally if he could have reached the ball to play it.

Your attempt to give your opponent access must not be made after a delay to hide the ball using your body – it must be immediate. (You can, of course, disguise and conceal your shot when you are the incoming striker, though.)

The word 'direct' is important here. Your opponent should be able to

Player A has played a bad shot which is returning on a line between himself and the 'T'. He must not cross that line if, in doing so, he is obstructing player B's view of the approaching ball or his shot at it. Stroke to B.

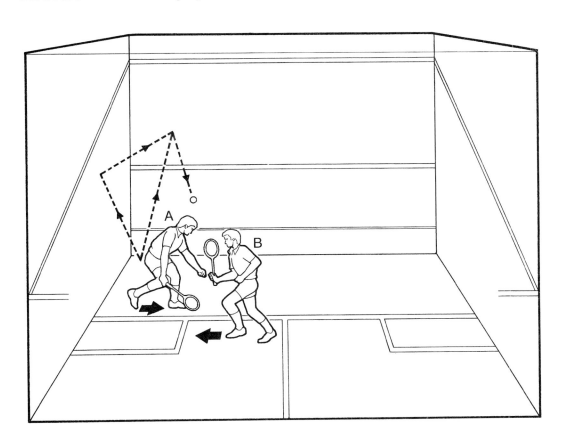

reach the ball in a straight line, with you having peeled off in an arc back to the 'T'. The route must take account of the precedence of direct movement to the ball by the incoming player.

If you provide room for access, but the incoming player does not take the direct route and does not reach the ball because of your obstruction of his indirect route, it is considered that he has 'created his own interference'. There was no reason for him to take the circuitous route, and so a let would not be allowable.

In this match between two top English international players, Cassie Jackman (right) strayed too close to opponent Fiona Geaves as she was about to play the ball, forcing her to stop. A stroke was awarded to Geaves.

Another common situation is where a player guesses wrongly where his opponent is going to hit the ball, and starts moving the wrong way. When he changes direction to reach the ball and is then obstructed by the opponent, a let may be played – but only if he could have reached the ball.

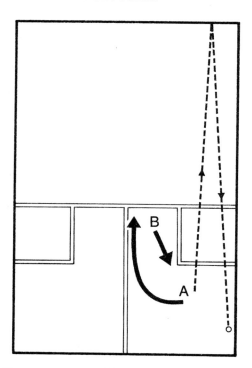

Player movement. After striking the ball, player A returns to the 'T' in an arc to give his opponent, player B, direct access to the ball. Clearly, if A were to move straight back to the 'T' he would interfere with B's line to the ball.

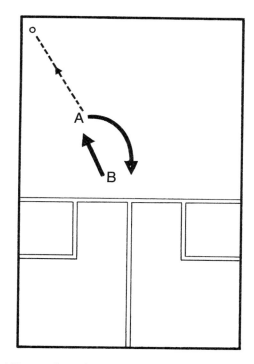

When a drop shot is played, player A must move away from it to allow a direct route for player B. 'Standing on a shot' (not clearing away from it) can result in a stroke being awarded to the incoming player.

It could not be a stroke because the original route was not blocked.

This is a fundamental facet of play, and one which leads to decisions being required on a regular basis. It is discussed further on p. 33.

Freedom of stroke

The follow-on to giving your opponent access to reach the ball is to place yourself far enough away from him so that he has room for a reasonable racket swing. A player may not 'crowd' a backswing or follow-through by

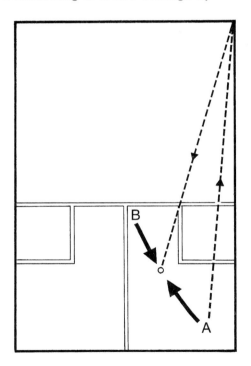

When the ball comes between player A and player B (often after a straight drive that comes out of the front-wall nick), then if A runs into the swing of B, a stroke will be awarded to B (see p.40).

being too close. If he does, the striker can expect a stroke if he is unable to make or complete his swing. However, the backswing and follow-through cannot be especially wide, with the arm held straight and wrist not cocked.

It should also be noted that a let or stroke cannot be awarded if a player strikes his opponent with the racket on the follow-through, and claims that this interference caused his shot to go down or out of court, as the ball had already been struck before contact.

Clear front wall

So, you have moved out of the path of your incoming opponent and not crowded his swing; but there is still one more responsibility that remains with you. You must give him the opportunity to hit towards any part of the front wall directly. Very often a player will move aside, but only enough for the player behind to hit the ball down the nearest side wall. Any cross-court shot would hit his opponent on the way to the front wall. By playing the ball in this situation you would very often put yourself at a disadvantage. Technically, if your opponent remains in the line of any part of the front wall, owing to not having made enough of an effort to clear the ball, he loses the rally if you refrain from playing the ball.

In practice, your opponent will probably not even realize that he has been blocking part of the front wall, or that he must not do so. Therefore, it can often be best to ask for a let on the basis of possible danger while gently explaining that it is actually a stroke you can call for. If he persists in not clearing fully, you may then have no option but to claim the strokes that you are entitled to.

Many of the great 'blockers' are often comparatively inexperienced players who can be bracketed together under a group title of 'front wall starers'! If they hit the ball to the back, they plant their feet squarely across the 'T', legs lightly bent, looking fixedly at the front wall, waiting for the ball to come into view as it reaches the front.

Very often they have simply not realized that their rear remains in the firing line for any cross-court shot. They also have not realized that, by not watching their opponent, they have dramatically cut down their reaction time, as they see the ball so much later. Players who do this need to be gently told of the problem that they are creating.

However frustrated you get if your opponent fails to give you a full view of the front wall, do not hit him with the ball, even softly, to make the point. He only needs to look round and the ball could hit him in the eye.

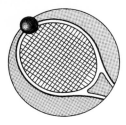

LET, NO LET AND STROKE

As has already been stated, the whole purpose of the rules is to help bring about a fair result to any match, and help to keep squash as safe as possible. With common sense and both players making every effort to get out of the way when they are not striking, games can be played with very little recourse to decisions which will resolve any unfinished rallies. However, there will always be those occasions when the ball passes close to a player or a collision takes place.

Then what happens? Is it a 'let', which means starting the rally again? Or is it a 'stroke' to one player, which means the point is awarded to him?

● 'LINE OF THINKING'

The thought processes that referees use to make these decisions are called the referee's 'line of thinking'(see diagram opposite) and are the ones that all players should study and commit to memory. Whatever your standard of play, it will be applicable to your game. It may seem a little complicated, but if you apply it to a match you watch, or a video of a professional championship, you will see that it has universal application.

Try thinking of a situation that took place in your last game, and start at Question 1. Then move progressively along the appropriate arrows till you reach a decision. It could be that this step-by-step approach gives a decision at Question 1, but it may not be until all four questions have been responded to that a decision is reached.

Question 1 Did any form of interference actually occur?

Interference, or obstruction as it is often called, occurs when your opponent remains in the way and so

THE REFEREES LINE OF THINKING CONCERNING INTERFERENCE

QUESTION   **DECISION**

1 Did any form of interference actually occur?

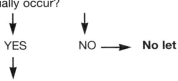

YES   NO ⟶ **No let**

2 Could the obstructed player have reached the ball and made a good return, and was he making every effort to do so?

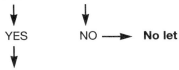

YES   NO ⟶ **No let**

3 After making his shot, what was the obstructing player doing? Was he making every effort to get out of the opponent's way?

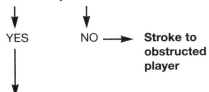

YES   NO ⟶ **Stroke to obstructed player**

4 Was the obstructed player prevented from playing a winning shot?

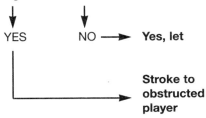

YES   NO ⟶ **Yes, let**

⟶ **Stroke to obstructed player**

prevents you from reaching the ball. This means a genuine difficulty which causes you problems, rather than a very slight readjustment that does not prevent you from continuing the rally if you wish to do so.

There are a few situations which occur regularly and constitute interference. They include:

• you run into your opponent as you move towards the ball
• your opponent runs into you as he moves away from his shot
• you take evasive action to prevent colliding or being tripped by your opponent
• your opponent has hit the ball back close to himself so is shielding it from you
• your swing is restricted because you are crowded
• your opponent's body does not give you the opportunity to hit the ball to any part of the front wall.

When any of the above occur, you must stop immediately, i.e. before going on to hit the ball, and ask for a let. If you carry on and then stop when you realize that the ball is more difficult to hit than you thought, or you actually complete the shot, then it is too late. You cannot have it both ways – you either stop or carry on.

Additionally, you must remember that you are obliged to make every effort to play the ball, so you should not stop for some very minor or imagined interference, as a referee would not award you a let were you to

Egyptian Ahmed Barada will claim that world number one Jansher Khan has not moved out of the way sufficiently!

do so in an officiated match. If you accept that slight contacts, a certain amount of moving around your opponent and some readjustment of route will always be part and parcel of squash, then the game will be less 'stop-start', and ultimately more satisfying for both players.

If a situation as described above has occurred and play has halted, we can progress to the next stage in the line of thinking.

Question 2 Could the obstructed player have reached the ball and made a good return, and was he making every effort to do so?

If there has been interference, we must now look at the incoming player's situation in two ways:

- could he have returned the ball if the interference had not occurred?
- was he making every effort to reach the ball?

Player B cannot claim a let if he is unable to readjust in order to reach the ball played by A.

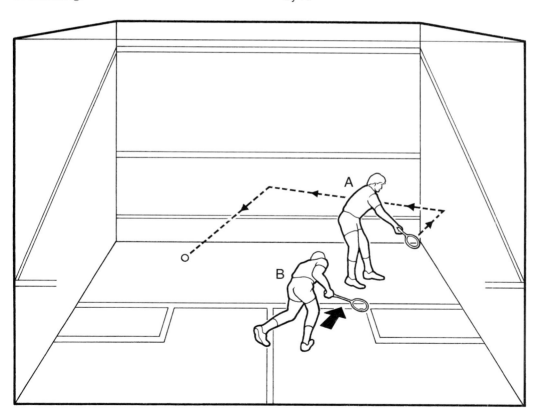

The first point takes us back to the fundamental principle of a fair result to the rally in question. This means that the incoming player has no right to expect a let based upon interference if he simply could not have continued the rally had there been no problem.

You cannot use this rule when your opponent has played such a severe or well-positioned shot that you would have been defeated by it. A dead nick or a perfect length, for example, cannot be negated by a claim for a let. Similarly, there is no legitimate appeal if your opponent's drop shot would have bounced twice before your gallop to the front wall enabled you to reach it. In these instances you must accept that the rally is lost even though interference has taken place, and move across to receive service for the next rally.

Point two brings in the 'making every effort' criterion. You have no right to stop play and ask for a let if the interference has been so slight that you could quite easily shrug it off and continue without undue difficulty. As mentioned before, while squash is not a contact sport in the sense of major impact such as rugby, it is inevitable that players will brush past each other, and these buffetings should be ignored except when they significantly affect your ability to reach and to hit the ball.

Also, importantly, you are not permitted to use your opponent's proximity to avoid running for a

difficult shot. Simply moving into the back or side of your opponent and asking is known as a 'lazy let', and would not be allowed by a referee.

However, it should be emphasized that, while you are supposed to make every effort to reach the ball, you are certainly under no obligation to run headlong into your opponent to prove that you are doing so – quite the reverse. When you are obstructed, try to stop before any unnecessarily forceful physical contact has taken place.

Now that we have progressed along the line of thinking and agreed that the answer to Question 2 is 'yes', we move to the next proposition.

Questions 3 and 4 After striking the ball, did you make every effort to get out of your opponent's way?
You have no right to stand still admiring your shot, or to watch your opponent try to reach it! If there is any prospect of the incoming player being able to reach the ball, then if you do not try hard to get out of his way the stroke is awarded against you. (Note that the incoming player must be able to reach the ball before it bounces twice. If he cannot do so – is stranded at the wrong end of the court, perhaps – then if you hit the ball close to yourself and don't clear it you would still win the rally.)

Also, while you are permitted to make life more difficult for your opponent by 'shielding' the ball while you are playing (i.e. positioning your body so that it is more difficult for him to see), once the shot has been completed you must get out of the way, and not continue to disallow him a view of the ball.

Finally, even if your body is out of the way, if your racket remains in a position which prevents your opponent from playing a winning shot, then the stroke is given to the obstructed player.

● SOME SPECIFIC EXAMPLES

Hitting your opponent with the ball
Should you hit your opponent with the ball during a rally the outcome will depend on where the ball was travelling to when its flight was interrupted (see also pp. 46–8):

- if it would not have reached the front wall then you lose the rally, as you would have done so had it not struck your opponent
- if it was on its way directly to the front wall then your opponent loses the rally (you will recall that it is the obligation of the player to give you freedom to strike directly any part of the front wall)
- if it had hit the side wall, or was on its way to the side wall then, as long as it would have
- subsequently reached the front wall before bouncing, a let is played.

'Making every effort' does not include removing your opponent bodily from your route to the ball!

Remember the first rule of safety though – if there is any danger of hitting your opponent with the ball, refrain from playing and claim a let or stroke, as appropriate.

Second attempts to play a ball
If your opponent is unable to play his intended shot, or misses the ball, and has another attempt by chasing back and reaching the ball either before or after the ball has rebounded from the back wall, as long as you have given room for the initial attempt, irrespective of where the ball would have gone, a stroke cannot be awarded

if your opponent hits you with the ball – even if it was going directly to the front wall. In all situations of further attempts, a let is played, rather than a stroke, if necessary.

Turning

This is one of the more messy and dangerous situations which can occur in squash. In essence, turning means allowing the ball to pass one side of you, and then playing it on the other side, probably after it emerges from the back wall. There is always danger inherent in this manoeuvre because the change of direction often leaves the opponent exposed in the line of fire of the next shot.

There are two types of turning: 'actual', when the player physically rotates following the ball, and hits it from the other side of his body; and where the ball passes around the player, i.e. the player anticipates the trajectory of the ball and waits without actually following the ball round. Both are treated the same in terms of the rules, and can only result in a let.

Turning is not barred in squash, nor is it necessary to shout 'turning' as some players believe, but it can be dangerous for the opponent who will find it difficult to remain out of the way and so should be avoided, if possible. Certainly, if you feel the need

Sometimes the decision is simple. When a player hits the ball back close to himself, and his opponent is in position to play the ball, a stroke will be awarded to the incoming player.

to 'turn' during a rally, you must be even more mindful of the possibility of hitting your opponent with the ball, and be especially prepared to refrain from striking if necessary.

Finally, remember that you should always refrain from hitting the ball if your opponent may be in danger.

Shaping to play the ball

The word 'shaping' can be taken to suggest 'getting ready'. It means moving your feet, body and the racket into the start of the coil which will unleash itself onto the ball (it is not the act of actually playing the ball). Its significance is in the statement of intent, i.e. this is what I plan to do. Sometimes, though, you may change your mind, or you could even miss the ball. This will have an effect on the decisions that need to be taken if the rally is not concluded.

While we have already covered the fact that your opponent has an obligation to make room for you to reach and play the ball, this access may be difficult to provide if you require a second attempt to get to it:

- if you swing at and miss the ball, and your opponent then gets in the way of your route to the back wall, a let is the probable outcome
- if you swing at and miss the ball, and the ball then hits your opponent as he waits behind you, you are entitled to a let (not a stroke) if you could have recovered to make a good return; if you could

not have done so, your opponent wins the stroke

- if you do not make an attempt to hit the ball (possibly having shaped to play it, but decide not to), and the ball hits your opponent behind you, then he loses the stroke because he should not have been there; and your ability to have made a good return is not relevant.

However, if a return does not go where intended, accidental interference can still result in a stroke being awarded.

The most usual occurrence is when an intended straight drive down the side wall hits the front/side wall nick and pings across towards the 'T' instead. This forces the incoming player to change direction, but if he is fast enough to do so and the opponent is in the way then it is a stroke situation, despite him having originally intended to react to the drive (it can be justified simply on the basis that it was the poor shot of the opponent that created the situation). It is not a further attempt by the incoming player, and is simply covered by 'interference', as discussed earlier.

● JUMPING OVER THE BALL

The rules do not disallow players from jumping over the ball to avoid being hit by it. If the opponent is not able to

reach the ball you will still win the point. However, if your opponent is positioned behind you, then your evasive action will be in vain if he could have hit the front wall directly had he not refrained from striking. A stroke will be awarded to him.

● DISTRACTION

With so much that can be happening on the court and nearby, it is inevitable that occasionally a player will be put off in some way during a rally. These occurrences can be grouped under the term 'distraction' and will normally (though not always) result in a let being played. Overall, distractions can be split into three groups, i.e. those caused by your opponent, on your court, and nearby.

Caused by your opponent

If the distraction is accidental, e.g. your opponent noisily trips or sneezes, or generally makes an unexpected noise just as you are about to play your shot, if you refrain or stop during the execution of your stroke, then a let can be played.

If you are deliberately distracted, e.g. if your opponent attempts to put you off by shouting, stamping, etc, this falls within the 'player conduct' area and a referee would probably feel it necessary to award a stroke, as well as warning the player about his behaviour. (An example of stamping could be where you were stranded at the back of the court with both the opponent and ball at the front. A drop shot that you are a court length away from reaching would be the obvious conclusion of the rally. You stamp your feet in a pretence of moving rapidly up the court in the hope that your opponent will alter his shot to a lob or drive to the back, where you languish. This is a distraction which falls outside the scope of fair play.)

A player cannot distract his opponent by calling or shouting (other than asking for a let; see below) during a rally. Were a player to do so, it would probably result in a stroke being awarded to the opponent. A player may call 'let, please' or 'appeal, please', which immediately stops the rally for the situation to be dealt with, but no other calls may be made.

However, the call will not cause a let to be played if your opponent calls just *after* you have struck a ball that will hit the tin or go above the out line. In these instances, the intention to create a fair ending to the rally demands that you lose the point despite the call.

Note: if the distraction occurs *as* you are playing your shot (and so are unable to stop), then it is justifiable to ask for a let if it caused you to hit the ball into the tin or go out, but only if it was the distraction and not the poor execution of the shot which was to blame!

On your court

If an object falls from the gallery during a rally, this will result in a let being played, as the noise is likely to distract the players. However, if one player has clearly *already* hit a winning return, he wins the stroke. Similarly, a ball may loop over from an adjoining court; this, again, will probably distract the players and result in a let.

Should any of the above occur, and not be noticed until after a rally is concluded, then a let is not applicable, as there has been no actual distraction. An obvious example of this might be a piece of paper floating down into a back corner while a rally is being concluded at the front.

When an object does fall into the court, play should stop immediately so that the item can be removed, and any possible danger from it averted.

Nearby

If, for example, an alarm goes off, a baby screams or a tray is dropped, and a genuine distraction is caused, then play should stop, and a let be played when calm resumes. The two important factors related to this are:

- the distraction must be genuine – a slight disturbance that really does not affect your ability to continue the rally should be ignored
- stop play immediately – you must instantly stop at the time of distraction, as you are not permitted to stop later and refer back to something that occurred earlier.

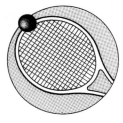

COLLISION AND INJURY

Bodies, rackets and balls swirling around inside the rectangular box are inevitably going to lead to contact being made in various ways. While the rules are framed in such a way that damaging incidents are minimized, they do also deal with the outcomes should collisions occur.

Collisions on court fall into the following overall categories:

- being hit by a racket
- being hit by the ball
- players colliding.

● BEING HIT BY A RACKET

This section can be subdivided into:

- running into a backswing
- hitting the opponent on a backswing/follow-through
- excessive swing.

Running into a backswing

We have already covered the requirement that each player has to get out of the way and allow his opponent the freedom to play his shot. Clearly, this extends to the backswing, so if you hit a shot then move into your opponent (even if you are actually trying to vacate the area) your opponent wins the stroke.

Technically, referees in this situation would use the term 'failing to make every effort'. What is being suggested is that, since you have hit a shot which puts you in a bad position, such as getting caught up in your opponent's backswing, you have clearly failed to make every effort to avoid interference by actually causing it yourself.

The exception to this would be if the incoming player takes such a wide swing (with arms and racket fully extended) that you cannot get out of

A collision on which the referee will have to make a ruling.

42

the way, although you would have been able to do so if a bent arm had been employed. In this situation a let should be played.

Hitting the opponent on a backswing/follow-through

If your racket catches your opponent while you are on a backswing and you stop the swing, then the rally will normally be replayed – a let (unless your opponent is crowding you). However, very often because the motion is very swift and 'one-piece', the shot is made before a let is called. This is fine if you call before the ball hits the front wall, but what if it hits the tin or goes out? Or if you find subsequently that you have hit a winner?

It is not possible to offer one all-embracing answer that covers these situations in a comprehensive manner. Variations in the situations cause each to be viewed separately. Some guidance may be helpful, though:

- if you could have stopped and didn't, then you have no right to a second chance
- if you were caught, but it made no difference to the shot, then you should not ask for a let if the ball goes down or out – it is not sporting to do so

French player Julien Bonetat appears to be backpedalling to avoid running into Peter Nicol's swing, but if he is unable to clear fully then he will lose the stroke.

- your opponent should also take a sporting attitude and offer a let even if he believes the contact has been slight
- in the absence of a referee, it is very difficult to claim that your opponent has an excessive swing; it really is incumbent on you to recognize this and give him a wide berth, frustrating though this may be
- with regard to follow-through, though this would not normally affect the shot itself, it is still up to the incoming player not to 'crowd', that is he should give you room to complete the swing; you do not have a right to move into the follow-through of your opponent as he completes it (indeed it is a right that you would hardly wish to have as it could lead to injury!).

Excessive swing

The principal point from the point of view of safety is that all players are required to restrict the length and width of their swing to avoid danger to the opponent, as far as possible. A referee, if present, would make a ruling on whether a swing was excessive.

Players do have the right to raise the racket and delay their swing. If the ball is slow enough for a player to move backwards with it he can do so, even if it means that the opponent has to continue to keep moving out of the way. If he does not make every effort to keep clear, or is prevented from doing so by the back or side wall,

The referee must decide whether an excessive swing has prevented reasonable access for the incoming player.

a stroke is then awarded under the obstruction rule.

What a player cannot do, however, is to hold out the racket purely to impede his opponent, without actually shaping to play the ball.

● BEING HIT BY THE BALL

It has already been emphasized that safety is paramount, and that players must refrain from striking the ball if the opponent is in the way. But what if he unexpectedly moves into the flight

of the ball? Yes, he may have a livid bruise, but what is the outcome in terms of the rules?

The diagrams opposite neatly sum up the options that are applicable.

It is important to stress that in all the cases shown the outcome is the same if the player refrains from playing on the basis that the ball would have hit the opponent, so you do not have to actually hit him to be given a stroke, if applicable.

If the ball was going to hit the front wall directly, and it is not a 'second attempt' and no 'turning' has occurred, a stroke is awarded. There are also situations where a let is the correct conclusion, and where no let is applicable. The last is likely to occur where, for example, a player attempts a desperate boast (where the ball hits the side wall before going onto the front wall) from the back corner, which only succeeds in coming off the side wall and hits the player waiting on the 'T', but with no chance of the ball ever reaching the front wall before bouncing.

Ordinarily, if a player hits the ball against the front wall only for it to return and hit him he loses the rally. The exception to this is if he attempts to evade the ball, and would have succeeded had he not been blocked by his opponent. A let would be played in this instance unless the opposing player was prevented from making a winning return.

The rally is still lost by a player when he gets hit by his own shot, even if the opponent is stranded elsewhere

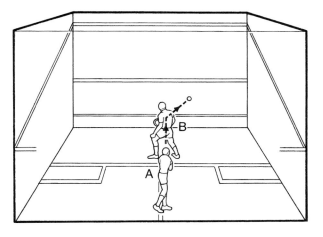

Player A has hit player B with the ball, with what would have been a good return going directly to the front wall. Stroke to B.

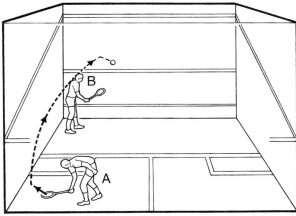

Player A has hit player B with the ball, having hit it against the back wall. A let is then called, as the ball was not going directly to the front wall.

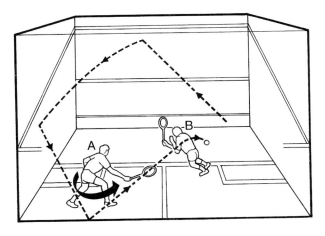

Player A has hit player B with the ball, after 'turning'. A let is called, even though the ball was going directly to the front wall.

in the court, for example when you play a drop shot when your opponent is sprawled against the back wall, only for it to hit your foot after coming off the front wall.

PLAYERS COLLIDING

It is inevitable that players will sometimes brush past each other in the course of a rally, and at times contact will be even more substantial. If a player cannot continue after the contact, but would have been able to reach and play the ball, the provisions of the interference rules then apply. Generally, a let will be played. The essential point is that play should stop immediately. A let cannot subsequently be claimed at the end of a rally for previous contact.

I make no apologies for reminding players here that unnecessary physical contact is prohibited.

A referee, if present, could award conduct penalties for any of the infringements listed below. Irrespective of these provisions, players should avoid these excesses at all times.

- Players should not push off each other
- Players should not 'run through' an opponent who is in the way
- Players should not barge into their opponent.

At times it may be tempting to make contact with an opponent just to emphasize to him that you think he is continually making too little effort to get of the way. As a player you should refrain from doing so, and as a referee you should acknowledge what is occurring by penalizing the player who is not making an effort, as appropriate.

Above Sometimes it looks as if both players are going to play the same shot, and often the referee has to decide whether the incoming player is interfering with his opponent while he is completeing his shot.

Opposite 1996 World Open Champion Sarah Fitzgerald (left) brushes past Fiona Geaves, but not enough to interfere with her completed stroke, so the rally continues.

Here Peter Nicol (Scotland) plays a short ball with Jansher Khan (Pakistan) trapped behind him. It is Jansher's responsibility to move around his opponent rather than through him, as he attempts to reach the ball.

 # INJURY

Injuries are divided into three categories for squash classification:

- self-inflicted
- contributed
- dangerous play (inflicted by the opponent).

In a match situation, once the referee has determined what has caused the injury, then different courses of action follow.

Self-inflicted injury
This form of injury embraces cuts and grazes (blood flow) on court, pulled muscles, other injuries occurring when tripping or falling (where the opponent is not involved), or being hit by the racket of the opponent when getting too close, i.e. crowding. Other than the last, these are injuries where the opponent has not contributed, and in all cases the opponent is free of blame.

In a match, a player has a period of three minutes in which to recover. If at the end of this time the player is still unable to continue, he must either gain extra time by forfeiting the next game and so have the time between it and the following one, or concede the match. Only one game may be concluded by a player in this manner. Additional recovery time may be allowed by the referee if blood flow is involved.

For example, if a player suddenly feels that he is going to be sick, he can forfeit the game in progress and leave the court to do so, as long as he returns within the specified time frame. However, a player immediately forfeits the match if he is actually sick on the court, as he is therefore responsible for rendering the court unplayable.

Contributed injury
This involves an on-court injury where both players have accidentally contributed to a situation, where no blame can be attributed exclusively to one player, for example a collision or a racket-inflicted injury in which neither crowding nor excessive swing have played a part.

In a match situation, a standard one-hour recovery time applies, but this can be extended, depending on the circumstances. These are governed by general court availability and the schedule of the competition.

Normally, the match would restart at the score reached when the accident occurred, except where it resumes on the following day, in which case if both players agree it can start from the beginning again. If the injured player is unable to resume, he would then concede the match.

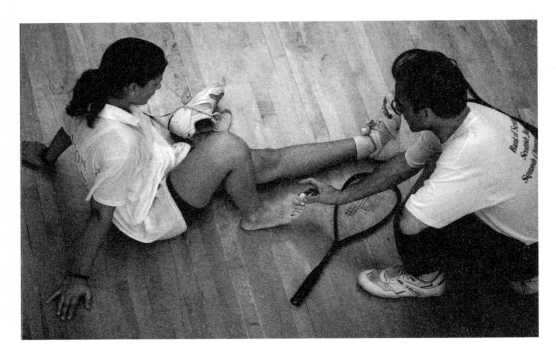

Dangerous play (inflicted by the opponent)

A player may become injured because of his opponent's dangerous play or his disregard of the on-court conduct stipulations, or as a result of an accident where the opponent is fully to blame (even between rallies). Examples of this are:

- barging or pushing an opponent
- hitting an opponent while taking an excessive swing
- hitting an opponent with a racket as it slips from the hand
- hitting an opponent deliberately with the ball (when refraining was possible).

Once the referee has decided how the injury occurred, the course of action he must then take becomes clear.

In these instances, if the injured player is unable to continue, then he is awarded the match.

Bleeding on court

All players are required to leave court to stem blood flow and cover a wound. They should only return when the bleeding has stopped and some form of cover has been applied. This not only protects the opponent from transmission of infection, but also avoids the court being stained.

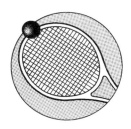

FAIR PLAY AND PLAYER CONDUCT

One of the enduring attractions of another sport – golf – is the sense of honesty that is instilled into the players early on. They are encouraged to point out their errors, whether noticed or not, and generally do. A code of self-regulation is fundamental for golfers. There should be a similar sporting attitude among squash players at all times, as there needs to be a certain amount of give and take, so that both players do not feel that their opponent is trying to gain an unfair advantage.

● FAIR PLAY GUIDELINES

The obvious maxim is 'when in doubt, play a let', but players should be ready to offer their opponent a stroke, too, when appropriate.

Here are a few guidelines to follow:

- only ask for a let if:
  – you have made every effort to play the ball
  – you could actually have reached it

- offer your opponent a stroke (not a let) if:
  – you run into his backswing or crowd him
  – you don't make every effort to get out of the way
  – you find yourself blocking a shot to the front wall

- always call your own ball down or out, even if you are not absolutely certain

- call your own service faults.

Do not wait for your opponent to claim – offer him what he is due.

● CONDUCT ON COURT

The referee has various warnings and sanctions in his armoury to deal with the whole range of situations which relate to player behaviour. These are called 'conduct' penalties. Because players generally behave in a mature and sportsmanlike manner, these penalties are not often called into use. When there are no match officials, the responsibilities of the two players on court are total in this regard.

Act in an unsportsmanlike, intimidating or other anti-social way and you will soon run out of opponents willing to go on court with you.

But what are the unbecoming manners and behavioural shortcomings that fall within the 'conduct' area? They include:

- swearing, and other audible and visible obscenities
- verbally abusing an opponent
- shouting during play
- intimidating an opponent
- unnecessary physical contact, e.g. barging
- deliberate dangerous play
- excessive racket swing
- abuse of racket or ball
- time-wasting between points
- arguing with the referee.

Any oafish or dangerous behaviour has no place on the squash court.

A referee may (1) warn a player, (2) award a stroke, (3) award a game, or (4) award a match against him for any of the above, or even for being offensive to officials or spectators in a way that brings the game into disrepute. The referee does not need to proceed individually through each increasingly severe penalty. He may start at any level, depending on the nature of what has occurred.

When you referee, to let the player know that an offence has been committed and that you have taken formal action, you would announce the appropriate call from the following.

- Conduct warning (player's name) for (offence)
- Conduct stroke (player's name) for (offence); stroke to (opponent's name)
- Conduct game (player's name) for (offence), game to (opponent's name)
- Conduct match (player's name) for (offence), match to (opponent's name).

Obviously it is essential to name the player against whom action has been taken in order to avoid uncertainty.

If you are called upon to referee at any time, you should remember that your responsibilities incorporate the area of conduct in addition to the general playing side, and you should not be afraid to warn a player about his behaviour, or take firmer action, if required. Indeed, your responsibilities include keeping order on the gallery. If necessary, you should not hesitate to ask any rowdy or abusive spectators to desist; and, if forced to do so, suspend play until they leave the viewing area.

Many players, spectators and especially parents are not aware that they are not allowed to coach players during the course of a game. This may only be done between games. Of course, encouragement may be offered between rallies (not during, as this would constitute a distraction) but to shout tactical advice or comment about the opponent is not permitted.

As can readily be seen, there is a great deal more to officiating than simply keeping score!

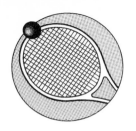

MARKING, REFEREEING AND KEEPING SCORE

For the two players careering about the court, making interpretive decisions such as 'Could a ball have been reached?' or 'Was there obstruction?' is not always easy. As players improve enough to play for club teams, they will find themselves being called upon to referee their fellow members; and, at a higher level still, will have the benefit of qualified officials who will take on the task of officiating their matches.

The officials in many sports have to determine whether a specific rule has been transgressed in relation to what has just taken place in front of them. However, squash officiating demands the ability to look into the future! The line of thinking extends to deciding what would have happened if the problem had not occurred. Would the ball have reached the front wall? Could the player have got to the ball? And so on.

These interpretative decisions make squash officiating a difficult task indeed. So when you read in the press that a professional player thinks that the match referee has got it wrong, just reflect that the player and referee are in very different physical positions in which to assess the situation. The referee may have years of international refereeing experience, and the player may have never even read the rules. That said, of course, referees do make mistakes, but at the highest levels far fewer than they are credited with.

● THE MARKER'S ROLE

Where there are two officials, the 'marker' is basically responsible for the scoring aspects, and so the flow of the game, while the referee is in overall control of the match, makes decisions and deals with appeals from players. If there is only one official, he will take on the role of both referee and marker.

The marker:

- announces the commencement of the match
- keeps the score
- calls the score
- calls down, out, not up, footfaults and other service faults
- repeats all decisions made by the referee
- (where he is the sole official) takes on the duties of the referee (see pp. 58–61).

Refereeing can be quite exhausting!

When marking, it is important to call scores and decisions loudly and clearly. You should also do so promptly, so that the players are not kept waiting at the point of service because you have not yet called the score. You should also attempt to memorize and get used to the correct calls so that the possibility of misunderstanding is minimized. The marker's calls are as follows.

- Footfault (on service)
- Fault (any other service fault – see p. 20.
- Out (when the ball hits a wall above the out line)
- Down (when the ball hits the tin or floor)
- Not up (double bounce, double hit or scoop)
- Set one (at eight all, when receiver decides to play to nine)
- Set two (at eight all, when receiver decides to play to ten)
- Game ball (when the server will win the game if he wins the next rally)
- Match ball (when the server will win the match if he wins the next rally).

It will help you to use the terms naturally as you call your own shots down, out, not up and so on in your own games.

The referee, who is responsible for time-keeping, will announce 'half-time' at the midpoint of the warm-up. Then, once the marker has found out from the players who is serving, he waits until they are ready to start and then announces the match, starting with the event itself, for example 'XYZ Event Quarter Final, Smith serving, Khan receiving, best of five games, love all'.

Later we will look at how the marker records the score, but in addition during each rally he will look at all shots in case a call is necessary (or to make a ruling if he is referee too). If a referee is present, then any call of the marker (or absence of one) can go to the referee on appeal; and the marker will also repeat decisions made by the referee before calling the score.

In the event of the score reaching eight all, the marker will enquire whether the receiver wants to play set one (to nine points) or set two (to ten points) and announce the player's decision accordingly.

If the marker is undertaking the officiating on his own, then he will take on the duties below in addition to those described above.

● THE REFEREE'S ROLE

The referee is in charge. It is his duty to ensure that the *Rules of Squash* are followed and that a fair result is achieved. To do this he has a wide range of powers. It is his judgement that prevails on all issues concerning the play, the court, timing, the ball and even spectators. He will respond to appeals, stop play if necessary and deal with conduct problems.

While at club level the referee tends only to keep the score and deal with the let/no let/stroke situations, he is actually responsible for a lot more besides. The referee:

- controls the running of the match
- deals with all appeals for lets etc
- deals with appeals made against marker's calls (and where a player appeals to suggest that the marker should have made a call)
- deals with the time-keeping and related calls.

Player appeals
A player may ask only for a let (by saying 'Let, please') even if he wants to be awarded a stroke. The calls you should employ when refereeing are:

- yes let – when you allow a let, following an appeal from a player
- no let – when you disallow an appeal for a let
- stroke to (player's name) – when you award a stroke (you must give the name of the player to whom you are awarding the stroke to avoid any uncertainty).

When refereeing, you should also remember that at no time should a referee offer a let. *Always wait to be asked*. Referees should bear in mind

The advent of glass back walls led to the introduction of purpose-built gantries for referees and markers.

that players sometimes make an appeal by gesture, or make no request assuming that it is blindingly clear that they wish to do so. In these instances, your best course if you are uncertain is to enquire whether they are actually making an appeal.

Should a player wish to enter into a dialogue, or explain further his request, it is important that the referee strikes the right balance between allowing this and the requirement that the match should proceed. Decisions don't need to be explained or defended, though a short explanation, followed by 'Please play on', may assist in concluding the debate.

Players may also appeal against a shot played by an opponent, believing there to have been a double bounce, double hit, scoop, down or out. Once the referee has determined exactly what the nature of the appeal is, then the response would normally be 'All shots were good' or 'I am not sure, play a let please'. If he were definitely to agree the appeal, the player might legitimately ask why he did not stop the rally at the time of the incident. It is the referee's responsibility to do so if he considers a service or return not good and there has been no call by the marker. The referee may also overrule a call made by a marker if he is certain in his own mind that an error has been made.

You should note that as a player if you raise your arm during a rally to indicate a doubtful shot of your

Seated on a gantry mounted on the back wall, a referee and marker have an unobstructed view of the play.

opponent, this is *not* an appeal. Your choices are to stop play and appeal immediately with the words 'Appeal please' or to continue the rally (a much wiser choice!) and to appeal at the end of the rally if you lose it. A raised arm has no meaning whatsoever under the rules, and the referee should be alert enough to know which shots are possibly questionable. As referee, if you think a shot is doubtful, you do nothing unless there is an appeal. Only then is the referee called upon to make a decision.

In all situations remember that the referee's decision is final.

While making the best possible decisions that you can is paramount, there are a few points that will definitely help you do so in a manner that will ensure you retain the appropriate level of authority and keep in the background as far as possible while the players go about their business.

- **Always make your decision promptly.** Players do not like a referee who appears unable to make a decision without extended mental re-runs of the evidence.
- **Speak loudly.** Players must be able to hear your calls and decisions.
- **Always sound positive.** If you have an air of confidence it conveys itself to the players.
- **Don't chat with those standing near you during a game.** Not only should you be concentrating, but the players should be able to see that you are.
- **Don't panic!** If a situation arises then the rules are there to provide an answer. If what happens seems to fall outside the scope of the rules, then use common sense as your yardstick.

Perhaps the next stage for you will be to take a refereeing course and become qualified. Even if you have no aspirations to referee any matches higher than the standard of your own playing level you will certainly find the course stimulating. Your national governing body office can provide you with details and contacts.

● HOW TO KEEP SCORE

Any player who has become involved in team squash will probably have encountered any number of differing styles of scoresheet. During the evening, as you stand on the gallery, a sheet and pencil will be thrust at you, accompanied by an instruction to officiate for team members on a given court.

We have discussed many details of the aspects involved when refereeing – always within the overriding precept of bringing a match to a fair conclusion. But just how is the score recorded on the way to this conclusion?

In fact there is no one recognized format that is universally recommended. All of the differing sheet layouts on pre-printed score pads are perfectly acceptable as long as the person concerned feels comfortable with them.

All methods start with the same formalities. The routine begins before the match itself starts, as it is important to complete the names of the players, the event and any other required information at the top of the sheet. If the names of the players have been written for you, check that the two players warming up are actually the correct ones!

It is also important that you have a watch, clock or stopwatch so that you can deal with timing elements, such as warm-up periods and the time allowed between games. Remember if you are the referee/marker (combined) or the referee, you will need to call out timing, e.g. 15 seconds (before the end of an interval between games).

Most scoresheet systems go vertically down the page, although one goes horizontally from left to right.

Five examples of scoring systems, all of which are equally valid.

The key things to bear in mind are that:

- scoresheets must be comprehensive in terms of necessary detail
- you should spend as little time as possible with your head down, writing
- it should be possible to refer/check the current position at a glance.

The diagram below shows a common layout. Note the information to be

Example 1		Example 2		Example 3		Example 4	
A	B	A	B	A	B	A	B
	OR	OR		0-OR	0-1R		0-OR
	1L	1L		1-OL	1-1L		1-OL
	2R		OR	1-4R	2-1R		2-OR
			1L	2-4L	3-1L	0-2R	
OR			2R	3-4R	4-1R	1-2L	
1L			3L	4-4L	4-4R	2-2R	
	2R	1L		4-7R	5-4L		2-2R
	3L (S)	2R		5-7L	6-4R		3-2L
1L		3L		6-7R	7-4L		4-2R
2R		4R			7-6R		5-2L
(X) 3L			3L (X)		8-8L	2-5R	
4R			4R			3-5L	
5L			5L				5-3R
(X) 6R		4R					6-3L
7L		5L					7-3R
		6R					8-3L
	3R	7L				3-8R	
			5L			4-8L	
7R			6R (S)				
8L			7L				
			8R				
		7R					
		8L	(2)				
		9R					
9	3	10	8	6	9	4	9

Example→ 5	A	RLR 012	RL 23		RL 34		LRL 456		RLR 678	9	
	B		0123 RLRL		345 RLR		567 RLR		78 RL	(1)	8

completed at the top. If it is helpful to you, before the match starts, you can cover the sheet in horizontal lines to assist in lining up the scores as each game progresses.

Let us now look at some examples of the ways in which you can complete the sheet. Each is acceptable, and all use some basic notation:

A = player name
B = player name
L = serving from left box
R = serving from right box
1 = set 1 (serving at 8–8)
2 = set 2 (serving at 8–8)
X = let played
S = stroke awarded

Example 1 As with all methods, you start by denoting who is serving first, and from which box. In this instance it is player B from the right box. Reading downwards, he has won the first two points before player A wins a rally and commences serving at 0–2 (from the right box).

Points to note are:

- a stroke is awarded to player B at 2–1
- player A serves again following lets at 3–3 and 6–3.

This system is easy to follow and involves the minimum of notation.

Example 2 This is very similar to example 1, except that use is made of

horizontal lines. Note that when player A won the rally at 7–8 to move to 8–8, player B called 'set 2'.

Example 3 This method involves writing both players' scores in the column of the current server, and crossing out the preceding score at the end of each rally. It has the benefit of requiring less space, but involves more writing at the end of each rally.

Example 4 This method is similar to that shown in example 3, but uses the downward gaps to save crossing through preceding scores.

Example 5 This presentation is similar to that of examples 1 and 2, but is presented horizontally, normally using small squares.

If you haven't scored a match, simply stand on the gallery and do so for a friend. After a little while the recording side will become very simple. Decision-making also can only improve with experience, but ease of scorekeeping will undoubtedly come first!

Copies of the full *Rules of Squash* are available from all national governing body offices or from the World Squash Federation, 6 Havelock Road, Hastings, East Sussex TN34 1BP (tel: (44) 1424 429245; fax: (44) 1424 429250).

INDEX